Injustice in the Working of the Education Act of 1870.

I0169087

A SPEECH

DELIVERED AT

THE ANNUAL MEETING OF THE ENGLISH CHURCH UNION

ON THURSDAY, JUNE 7, 1883

BY

HENRY TEMPLE, M.A. Oxon.

VICAR OF S. JOHN THE EVANGELIST'S, LEEDS
AND HONORARY CANON OF RIPON.

PUBLISHED BY SPECIAL REQUEST.

RIVINGTONS

WATERLOO PLACE, LONDON

AND ENGLISH CHURCH UNION OFFICE, 35, WELLINGTON STREET, STRAND

MDCCCLXXXIII

PREFATORY NOTE.

THE figures contained in this speech are drawn chiefly from the memorial recently presented to the Prime Minister by the National Society, and the correctness of the statements in that memorial has been assumed throughout.

INJUSTICE IN THE WORKING OF THE EDUCATION ACT OF 1870.

As you are aware, Mr. President, it is not a member of the English Church Union, but one personally invited by yourself to address it, who now moves the resolution which stands in my name. Yet in undertaking this task, I feel that I am but discharging a small instalment of a very large debt which I owe to this Society. Ten years ago I had the honour of being requested to act as Secretary for the Northern Province to the promoters of that great meeting in S. James's Hall, which did, I believe, under God, effect something towards preserving to the English Church the use of the Athanasian Creed. I never shall forget, sir, how at that time you were good enough to place at my disposal the entire organization of this great Society, and how, by its help, a task which would have been Herculean in its dimensions, if not absolutely impracticable, became comparatively easy. The resolution before me is this :—

"That Board Schools should supplement, as far as possible—that is to say, in respect of secular teaching—not supplant, denominational schools; and that any legislation or any administration of the law which ignores this principle is faulty, and ought to be amended."[1]

When Mr. Forster first introduced that famous Bill which was afterwards licked into shape as the Education Act of 1870, he used these words: "On the one hand we acknowledge and make the utmost possible use of present educational efforts . . . ; on the other hand we assert in the strongest language that it is the duty of Government to take care that in every locality throughout the kingdom elementary education is provided by help of local agency." Speaker after speaker, in the course of the debates which ensued, echoed this same doctrine, Mr. Mundella, among others, asserting most strongly with respect to the then existing denominational schools that no statesman could for a moment dream of diminishing their utility or sweeping them away. So far as rating goes, the original Bill, as introduced by Mr. Forster, provided that the rate in the first instance should not exceed threepence in the pound ; and that whenever it reached that amount it should be supplemented, between the sums of threepence in the pound and ten shillings per scholar, by an extra grant from Government. Anything beyond ten shillings per scholar was set down to pure local extravagance, and I suppose would fall upon the rate again. But, in fact, threepence was deemed to be the utmost

[1] The resolution is here printed in the form in which it was passed, *i.e.* as amended by the Archdeacon of Taunton.

limit, excess over which was regarded as improbable, chimerical, Utopian. *Mais nous avons changé tout cela.* We know a great deal better now. The average for the whole country is now $5\frac{1}{2}d.$ in the pound. Half a crown in the pound is by no means an unknown figure. You in London are paying sevenpence in the pound, and some of us in Yorkshire considerably more. Of 2089 School Board districts in England and Wales, there are only 355, or less than 17 per cent., in which the rate does not exceed the extreme limit anticipated by Mr. Forster. The education rate of the country, exclusive of administration expenses and repayment of building loans, reaches £800,000 a year.

Now, what I wish to make clear to-day is, that of this £800,000 Churchmen have to pay the larger proportion, to support a system of elementary instruction which they barely tolerate and do not at all conscientiously approve ; while at the same time, for the sake of another system which they do approve, they have taxed themselves to the extent of nearly £12,000,000 for the erection of schools, for the working expenses of which they are further taxing themselves in the form of voluntary subscriptions to the tune of £600,000 a year. This, it appears to me, however Churchmen may be upborne by their religious principles in enduring it, cannot be regarded by them as other than a great hardship ; and no wonder if the cry is sometimes raised, " Why should not those who are thoroughly satisfied with the School Board system have the privilege all to themselves of supporting it, leaving the resources of those who prefer the denominational system free for the promotion of such teaching as they really approve ?"

Let us look for a parallel. According to the ancient law of England, the fabrics of our churches were kept in repair by means of a rate levied on the parishioners in respect of landed property which they had inherited or otherwise obtained, knowing that it was, and from time immemorial always had been, subject to this impost. Dissenters raised a cry on the principle that it was hard they should pay for the repair of fabrics which they did not use, while at the same time they were supporting voluntarily other fabrics which they did use for the purposes of worship they sincerely valued. They did not then wish to have anything to do with parish churches or churchyards. They had not then advanced so far as to claim the use of these properties without contributing to their maintenance. They only wished to be let alone. Well, their cry was heard. Rightly or wrongly, many Churchmen recognized a certain reasonableness in it; and church rates came practically to an end. Having secured their own immunity, our friends then thought to make a raid on our position. Like a lady with strong convictions about the desirableness of a marriage settlement, they first laid down the principle, " What is mine is my own ;" and then annexed this appendix, " But mind, what is yours is to be mine." And so was invented a system of

rating which did certainly not exist from time immemorial, which had no hoary honours of antiquity,
which no owner of property in this country had ever
before been subject to, which had formed no pre-
vious condition of our land tenure, and the object of
which was to form schools from which all catechisms,
formularies, and other best means of indoctrinating
Christian children with the articles of the Christian
faith, should be purposely banished and excluded.
A system was thus to be paid for which did great
violence to the consciences of Churchmen, and the rate
in aid of which, instead of being the paltry farthing
or half-farthing in the pound which had formed the
church-rate grievance, has shown its power to rise
into the region of the practically limitless.

We bore all this, we who in days gone by, when
statesmen had first laughed at us, and then frowned
on us, and then grudgingly aided us, had raised by
voluntary subscriptions for school buildings wherein
the poor should be taught what they needed to
know no less a sum than £6,270,577. We bore
this new rating scheme, which proscribed the best
methods of teaching Christian faith and duty.
Nay, what is more, we even, under the special
circumstances of the day, acquiesced in its necessity.
We saw thousands upon thousands of untaught
children outside of and uncovered by all our
voluntary efforts. Being unable to reach these, we
were only too glad that the State should recognize
the duty of reaching them, and we regretfully

admitted that what the State did it should do on
its own conditions.   But, then, those conditions, as
stated at the time, involved, and were by all parties
thoroughly understood to involve, first of all, a
recognition of the work which denominational
schools had done ; and secondly, an assurance that
that work should be aided, and in no way super-
seded, by the State action of the future.

Cardinal Manning, in a powerful article con-
tributed by him to the April number of the *Nine-
teenth Century*, quotes from four separate speeches
of our present Prime Minister (Mr. Gladstone), who,
remember, was Prime Minister at that time also,
words which leave the first of these assertions
beyond the pale of doubt.   Of these four passages,
I will read you only one.   On the third reading of
the Bill, July 27, 1870, Mr. Gladstone, reviewing
the whole situation, spoke as follows :—

"It was with us an absolute necessity—a
necessity of honour and a necessity of policy—to
respect and favour the educational establishment
and machinery we found existing in the country.
It was impossible for us to join in the language,
or to adopt the tone, which was conscientiously
and consistently taken by some members of the
House, who look upon these voluntary schools,
having generally a denominational character, as
admirable passing expedients, fit, indeed, to be
tolerated for a time, deserving all credit on account
of the motives which led to their foundation, but

wholly unsatisfactory as to their main purposes, and therefore to be supplanted by something they think better. That is a perfectly fair and intelligible theory for any gentleman to entertain, but I am sure it will be felt that it has never been the theory of the Government."

Mr. Gladstone even went on to say, which the Cardinal does not quote, that he regarded the then existing machinery as a very "angel from heaven, as the spirit of Christianity, working in the minds of men, and producing a profound and deep desire not only to give religious knowledge, but every element of education of essential value. . . . As Christianity," he added, "since it came into the world has given a new character to secular philanthropy, so religious zeal has created, in this country especially, an amount of anxiety never before exhibited for the promotion of a sound secular education."

No wonder if a statesman, and the head of a Government which held such sentiments about the usefulness of voluntary schools, should hold out such hopes as he did hold out, and make such a promise as in effect he did make on June 16, 1870. Feeling that in presence of a new help which might become a formidable rival something must be done to enable the old schools to hold their own, Mr. Gladstone said, "We think that an addition to the present grant from the Privy Council to the voluntary schools, which may be taken at its maximum at fifty per cent., would fully gain that object. . . . Speaking roughly, it is said that the expense of educating a child in an efficient secular school is thirty shillings, of which it may be said one third is now provided by the Privy Council, one third from voluntary sources, and one third by payments from the children. We think that if to the third which is now dispensed, the half of the second third were added, subject to the strict conditions which I have described with regard to secular education, the voluntary schools would have no reason to complain."

There, then, we have the emphatic approval and promise for the future of the most responsible person in her Majesty's dominions. What have we done on the faith of such assurances? I will tell you. We have built 5238 new schools, in addition to the 6382 which we had before. We have provided accommodation for 1,020,294 scholars, in addition to the 1,365,080 which we could house before. The cost of these new schools in respect of their sites and erection alone has been £5,611,617. Of this sum, Government has paid £278,022, which leaves, as voluntary Church expenditure—for building alone, observe, not for maintaining the schools— £5,333,595. Maintenance has cost us, in voluntary subscriptions only, £8,463,519, of which Church-men have paid no less than £6,693,726.[1]

[1] A small correction might possibly have to be made in the *last two sets* of figures, as I have not the figures for 1882 before me, and have made an allowance for them.

This is what we have done in response to the assurances of those most deeply responsible for the Education Act of 1870. Now let us consider how far these assurances have been justified by the action of the then existing and the two succeeding Governments. On this head our complaint is, that the promise made to us has been "kept to the ear and broken to the hope." It has been kept in the letter, but grievously falsified in the spirit. The fifty per cent. has been given with one hand, but taken away with the other. The requirements of the Education Department have been so extended that, whereas in 1870 the yearly cost of instruction in Church schools was £1 5s. 7½d. on each of 844,344 scholars, the cost now (1882) is £1 14s. 9d. on each of 1,538,400 scholars. And that this is not the result of undue extravagance on the part of managers appears from the fact that the annual cost per child in our Board schools is £2 1s. 6½d. ; and though this be so, so far are the voluntary schools from being inferior in efficiency to the others that, while the School Board receives from Government, as the result of examination by the inspector, 14s. 5½d. per head for its children, the Church schools have received an average of 14s. 10½d.

And what has been the result of this pressure? and how has the Church borne it? The answers to these questions I quote from the latest Government Report.

" Some 959 schools, including 665 Church, 14

Wesleyan, and 197 British schools, have been transferred to School Boards under these minutes. Of the 61 schools transferred during the past year, 50 were Church schools, 2 Wesleyan, and 6 of the remaining 9 were in connection with the British and Foreign School Society. We have no definite information with respect to the number of schools made over to boards (section 19) by private managers. But many of this latter class, as well as of the schools formally transferred, had not previously been in receipt of annual grants, so that they contribute to the increased accommodation in aided schools which has been provided in the last few years."

To illustrate the spirit which still actuates Churchmen and other denominationalists, listen to this striking testimony :—

"It is a somewhat remarkable proof of the *bonâ fide* character of the great efforts which have been made under the voluntary system to meet educational deficiencies, and of the strong hold which that system has upon the country, to find that of the 7237 schools established with the aid of Government grants in the course of the last fifty years, not more than 153[1] have ceased to exist; while only 382 Church schools, built with such aid for 98,349 scholars, 10 Wesleyan schools for 3740 scholars, and

---

[1] Fifty-seven of the schools aided by the Treasury, and ninety-six of those aided by the Department, have been closed by their managers.

166 British and Undenominational schools for 57,022 scholars, have been transferred, under the Act of 1870, to the management of School Boards."

There is the grievance which has been recently stated to the Prime Minister by the National Society; and the resolution which I have the honour to move suggests, and (if its principle be a sound one) proves, that this grievance is real. Where, then, must we look for a remedy?

In the first place, I think it would be a fair concession to exempt all school buildings wherein elementary education only was provided from all local rates whatever, as is done with churches and Dissenters' meeting-houses. Besides this, which is a rating question, two others of the suggested remedies are, I think, perfectly feasible and perfectly in accordance with justice.

1. To limit the amount of school rates, leaving to the Education Department or some other authority the responsibility of disallowing any increase beyond a specified poundage. Why should the average cost of educating a child in a Board school exceed by 6s. 9½d. the cost of educating him in a denominational school, when Government returns show that the teaching is not a bit more efficient? Why should School Boards be allowed to spend £12 per child on their buildings, while Churchmen spend little more than £5 per child? This would be one remedy.

2. Another would be to charge a larger share of

the whole cost of education on the Imperial Exchequer, and less on local rates and voluntary subscriptions.

Let it be clearly understood, as Cardinal Manning puts it, that we do not ask one shilling from public funds for religious teaching. All we ask is, that secular learning may be subsidized by the State according to its value, whoever the givers of it may be. At present those who do nothing for themselves receive twofold aid, and those who tax themselves to the utmost receive nothing but what they earn. We do not in the least want the Education Act to be repealed, or even materially altered. We want to have it honestly and equitably administered. We want to have the minutes and codes and byelaws carefully examined, and, perhaps, a good many of them swept away. We want good work in secular education to be taken as the test of a good workman, and good results, however realized, to be duly recognized and paid for. Give but a fair field and no favour. Religious principles will then assert themselves, and constitute themselves, as they used to do and ought to do, the strength and the safeguard of our educational system.

www.ingramcontent.com/pod-product-compliance
Lightning Source LLC
Chambersburg PA
CBHW081455070426
42452CB00042B/2741